ENLIGHTENED DESPOTISM

FRITZ HARTUNG

1957
(Reprinted 1967)

PREFACE

It is a privilege for the Historical Association to have the opportunity of publishing this pamphlet by Professor Fritz Hartung, in an English version prepared by Miss H. Otto and revised by the present writer. The author, who was Professor in the University of Berlin from 1923 to 1949, and whose " Constitutional History of Germany from the Fifteenth Century to the Present Day " is a standard work, has long enjoyed an international reputation as an expert on the period of Absolutism; and the present essay should do much to clarify a subject about which, though it figures prominently in teaching in this country, a great deal of confusion often persists. In deference to English usage, the pamphlet has been given the title " Enlightened Despotism "; but the title of the German original is " Enlightened Absolutism ", and readers of the following pages will see (below pp. 6–7) that Professor Hartung adduces powerful arguments why the latter term is preferable to the former. The essay first appeared in the " Historische Zeitschrift " (vol. 180) in 1955, and the present version is published with the kind permission of the former Editor of the " Historische Zeitschrift ", Professor Ludwig Dehio, to whom our thanks are due. Its appearance in this English form may, I hope, be considered as a tribute—to which others will doubtless be added in due course—from historians in this country to Professor Hartung in view of the imminent celebration of his 75th birthday.

G. BARRACLOUGH

ENLIGHTENED DESPOTISM

SAINT AUGUSTINE once said: " If no one enquires of me, I know; if I want to explain to an enquirer, I do not know ". That is also the position of historians who have to deal with " Enlightened Absolutism ", or (as it is usually called in English) " Enlightened Despotism ". When, some forty years ago, lecturing on modern constitutional history, I had for the first time to deal with the subject in detail, it was still possible to treat it as a clearly defined and unambiguous notion. It was, in fact, the only stage which in the controversy about the periodization of absolute monarchy had practically never been the object of disagreement. However, had one looked more closely, it would soon have become apparent that agreement was largely superficial. Roscher, for example, the first historian to divide the era of absolutism into periods, and to single out Enlightened Despotism as a particular phase in it, had regarded Frederick William I of Prussia as an enlightened monarch, whereas Koser, who, about forty years later, examined and criticized Roscher's scheme, was reluctant (probably justifiably) to describe Frederick William as " enlightened ".

It is not surprising, therefore, that a time arrived when historians asked themselves what the essential character of Enlightened Despotism really was. What is remarkable is that this did not occur until 1928, when, in the course of the International Historical Congress at Oslo, the French scholar, M. Lhéritier, made a critical study of this " vague and confused " term. During his work on the Intendants at the close of the *ancien régime* in France, he had found that there was no special study of Enlightened Despotism in existence. He regarded it as a most urgent task that a bibliography should be compiled and an investigation made into the origin of the term. As Secretary-General of the International Committee of Historical Sciences he urged scholars of all countries interested in these problems, to try to find a solution.[1]

It is only natural that the contribution he was himself able to make to the solution of the problem, within the limits of a single lecture, was based purely on French conditions. According to Lhéritier, Enlightened Despotism was born in the sixties of the eighteenth century as a theoretical programme of reform based on the doctrines of the Physiocrats, and in his opinion it acquired special importance not only because Turgot, Louis XVI's famous reforming minister, was one of its supporters in France, but also because its leaders established contact with sovereigns of other countries—e.g. Catherine II of Russia—and influenced their methods of government.

But even Lhéritier was forced to admit that most of the sovereigns who are commonly regarded as representatives of Enlightened Despotism were not influenced by these theories; on the contrary, their activities for the most part occurred before the doctrine of " despotisme éclairé " had been enunciated. Nevertheless he thought he could establish certain traits which the theorists and the practitioners had in common, i.e. their striving for progress, for " enlightenment " in the narrower sense of the word, particularly the implementation of religious tolerance, their reforms of the educational system, improvements in legal procedure, rationalization and centralization of the administration, the raising of the standard of living of the working classes, particularly of the peasantry, and the improvement of the economic situation of the country.

Nevertheless, Lhéritier's arguments are not entirely satisfactory; for example, Frederick the Great, who is usually regarded as a typical representative of Enlightened Despotism, cannot be fitted into the framework of his scheme without serious qualifications. The inadequacy of Lhéritier's arguments, however, is most evident when we attempt to define the chronological limits of Enlightened Despotism; for then we find that many of the reforms which he ascribes to Enlightened Despotism had, in fact, been initiated by earlier governments which cannot be called " enlightened ". It might be replied that one of the most characteristic features of Enlightened Absolutism is the energy shown in the carrying through of reform plans, and that this energy was the inevitable result of enlightened thought; but this argument is contradicted by the fact that many attempts at reform under Enlightened Despotism encountered insurmountable obstacles even in their initial stages, and that it was only at the time of the French Revolution that many of the aims envisaged by the Enlightened

4

Despots were attained. For this reason Lhéritier himself was inclined to include Napoleon I, who made the achievements of the Revolution permanent, among the Enlightened Despots, although this means abandoning the time-limit ordinarily allotted to the era of Absolutism and Enlightenment. He even raises the question whether it is not possible to find traces of enlightened despotism in the government of Napoleon III and in some of the systems of government that arose after the First World War. Such arguments evidently destroy the conception of Enlightened Despotism as a particular period in the general course of history.

These observations are not intended as criticism of Lhéritier, since he himself did not regard his lecture as conclusive, but rather as a basis for further discussion, and suggested that a commission be set up with the task of making further investigations. This suggestion was readily accepted by the Congress in Oslo. A Commission was established and its members did good work during the ten years before the Congress met again in Zürich in 1938; in particular, two questionnaires were circulated, which yielded a wealth of new material.

On the other hand, the misgivings of Friedrich Meinecke, who doubted whether the investigators would be able to adhere strictly to the plan, like horses harnessed to a cart, were not entirely unjustified.[2] Anyone glancing through the articles on Enlightened Despotism published in vols. 5 and 9 of the Bulletin of the International Committee of Historical Sciences will be left with the impression that, far from clarifying, all they do is to complicate the issue. Where Lhéritier extended the period of Enlightened Absolutism forward into our own times, other scholars pushed it far back into the past. The princes of the Italian Renaissance and the iconoclastic emperors of Byzantium were put forward as enlightened despots—and so were Marcus Aurelius and Pericles. Even Solomon was mentioned, although this was rather an ironical interjection during the discussion in Zürich than a seriously intended statement. The geographical limitations also were widely extended. Besides the European monarchies which hitherto had been the focus of interest, not only republican Switzerland, but even states that lay far outside the European sphere of cultural influence, e.g. Turkey, India and China, were taken into consideration. Furthermore, the basic conception of Enlightened

Despotism was so far diluted in the course of discussion that it was in danger of losing its character as a period of history, and in particular of constitutional history, and of becoming simply a chapter in the history of the philosophy of the Enlightenment.

These considerations indicate the limitations besetting a work on history undertaken in common by scholars of various nations. It is possible to organize the preparation of the material, but no satisfactory result can be achieved by the simple addition of the details. This became evident in the concluding article, in which Lhéritier summarized the work of the Commission.[3] In the endeavour not to hurt anybody's susceptibilities—an attitude easily understandable and excusable, and perhaps even laudable in the Secretary-General of an international body— he was unable to get beyond a series of commonplaces.

Under these circumstances there are perhaps good grounds for another attempt to clarify the essential character of Enlightened Despotism.[4] In the first place, I would like to say a few words about the term itself, basing myself on conclusions reached by H. Reclam in an unpublished dissertation (Berlin 1943), written under my supervision. None of the princes whom we are wont to regard as the representatives of Enlightened Despotism, ever used this expression. But we find the terms " Despotisme éclairé " or " Despotisme légal " in the writings of the Physiocrats from about 1760 onwards. The first to use it in his letters was Diderot; Th. G. Raynal first employed it publicly, when in his *Histoire philosophique et politique des établissements et du commerce des Européens dans les deux Indes* (Vol. 7, 1770, p.202), he declared: " Le gouvernement le plus heureux serait celui d'un despote juste et éclairé ". But when, at the time of the French Revolution, the interest taken in the Physiocrats and in absolutism flagged, the term was again forgotten. In 1847 Roscher introduced the expression " Aufgeklärter Absolutismus " into scholarly terminology in an article on the various stages of absolutism; and, perhaps following the example of the Physiocrats, the phrase " Enlightened Despotism " was also used simultaneously. Koser and Treitschke employed the latter term as a synonym for Enlightened Absolutism, and German (and other) historians have followed their example in not differentiating between the two. In my

6

view it is preferable to use the expression "Enlightened Absolutism", since this agrees with the older tradition, common to the whole of Europe, of distinguishing clearly between Absolutism—i.e. a form of government which is not hampered by parliamentary institutions, but which voluntarily submits to laws and acknowledges the rights of subjects—and Despotism, which is equivalent to unchecked tyranny.[5]

If we are to obtain a true conception of the essential character of Enlightened Absolutism, we must keep to the commonly accepted sense of the word "absolutism", which signifies—as indicated above—a monarchical form of government, which is not limited in the exercise of its powers by the co-operation or consent of a national representative body or of other autonomous corporations. To include oligarchies or aristocratic forms of government under this heading is not relevant; nor does it extend to democratic tyrannies—whether dictatorial or caesaristic in character. Therefore I shall not speak of England, which was represented on the Commission, since Lhéritier did not wish to deprive it of the glory of having had an enlightened government, but which did not participate in the Commission's work, since the English scholars were proudly conscious that their country had already overcome royal absolutism before the beginning of the Enlightenment. Neither shall I mention Switzerland, which also according to its representative on the Commission, Liebeskind, had nothing to do with Enlightened Absolutism.[6]

When once we understand that the monarchical form of absolutism is an essential element in the conception which concerns us here, only the attribute "enlightened" still requires more precise definition. As a result of the work of the Commission, it is evident that it would lead us too far if we were to stretch the term "Enlightened Absolutism" to cover every attempt at reform that was supported by the authority of an absolute monarch. The endeavour to intensify the power of the State by increasing the efficiency of the administration and the army, by stimulating national economy and thereby augmenting revenues—i.e. by a policy of mercantilism—was so frequent and so natural a concomitant of absolutism as such, that it cannot be regarded as a special characteristic of Enlightened Absolutism, unless one is willing to grant the title of "enlightened" monarch not only to Frederick William I, but also (as Wittram does)[7] to Peter the Great, or unless one considers the entire policy of absolutism from the fifteenth century onwards as " une esquisse du despotisme éclairé ", as Lefèbvre has done.[8] A workable definition is only possible if we use the word " enlightened " in the sense in which it is generally used in historical terminology by scholars who are thoroughly aware of what is meant by the Enlightenment. In this sense I would define " Enlightened Absolutism " as a form of government strongly influenced by the philosophy, and particularly by the political philosophy, of the Enlightenment. This definition implies that it is not enough to examine theory only; and this was clearly demonstrated by the representative of Soviet Russia, Pokrovsky, who, during the discussion that followed Lhéritier's Oslo lecture—which had centred to a large extent on the French Physiocrats—objected that the enlightened ideas of Catherine II had had little influence on her practice of government, particularly during her later years. The book on the foundations of Enlightened Absolutism which P. Klassen published in 1929 independent of the work of the Commission, also shows how inadequate the one-sided consideration of the theoretical literature can be. The most beautifully elaborated proposals of scholars have seldom changed the world, and it was an essential feature of Enlightened Absolutism that it did not stop short at theoretical considerations, but—political practice being an integral part of its basic conceptions—attempted to improve existing conditions in the light of its new understanding.

By establishing the connexion between Enlightened Absolutism and the Enlightenment of the eighteenth century, we are not only able to define precisely its intellectual content, but we also obtain that clear chronological determination of its place in time, which is so essential in all historical investigation; furthermore, we can perceive the social and economic causes which led to its occurrence as an historical force. From this point of view Enlightened Absolutism takes its place as the concluding phase in the history of the hierarchical society of Estates, which had been handed down from the Middle Ages. It is the final stage because the adherents of the new doctrine had already begun to question the rightness and expediency of the traditional division of society into classes determined by birth, i.e. into a privileged aristocracy, a bourgeoisie, which in comparison with the former was underprivileged but was nevertheless free, and an unfree peasant class. They tried to alleviate the hardships and inadequacies of this social system, but they lacked the courage to draw the full consequences from their theories and to overthrow the existing social order.

It is therefore only with the conditions of this specific period that the following pages will deal. As far as theory is concerned, there is no ground for contesting the view that the characteristic doctrines of *Despotisme éclairé* developed in France in the sixties of the eighteenth century, as a political off-shoot of the economic doctrines of the Physiocrats. The basic idea of the " Physiocrats " is implied by their name. In opposition to the artificial and unnatural economic and social order prevalent in France at that period, where a mercantilist economic policy favoured industry at the expense of agriculture, they advocated what they considered to be a natural order. This natural order had as its foundation the liberty of the individual, particularly in its economic aspects, i.e. freedom to choose a profession, freedom to pursue economic activity as one thought best, freedom and security of property. Any interference with the natural development of economic life through measures taken by the state—e.g. the regulation of the corn-trade—and more generally all forms of state-interference, were rejected on principle, not only because they were contrary to the individual's natural right to freedom, but also because they were considered economically harmful. Gournay, one of the less known Physiocrats, summed up the programme of his school in the oft quoted words: *Laisser faire, laisser passer*; and of Quesnay, physician of Louis XV and founder of the school, the following story was told. When Louis asked him what he would do if he were king, he answered: " Nothing ". And when Louis then asked him who in that case would rule, his answer is said to have been: " The Laws ".

This attitude presupposed, of course, that the natural order of the Physiocrats was already in existence. However, since in fact this natural order had been undermined for many centuries, the State could not be content with the simple policy of *laissez faire*. On the contrary, despotic power was needed to restore the natural order, to remove everything that hindered the free development of productive forces, and to overcome all obstructions raised by those who were interested in preserving the

9

existing state of affairs. To be sure, this despotic power should not be arbitrary but "legal", and the law by which it was regulated should be the law of logic, the outcome of the logical evidence, i.e. harmony between enlightened thought and whatever practical measures were planned. In politics this law would have the same impelling force—and, therefore, the same despotic power—as the laws of Euclid in mathematics; and the task of the enlightened despot would be only "de reconnaître, de proclamer et de faire respecter le droit naturel et d'assurer l'ordre naturel". In order to carry through this task it was necessary that the executive power of the State should lie undivided in the hands of the monarch; for the Physiocrats trusted so implicitly in the victorious power of enlightenment that they advocated hereditary monarchy, without any restrictions, and rejected energetically anything like the division of power so widely discussed since the time of Montesquieu, or parliamentary control. On the other hand they demanded the right to free discussion.

Even foreign policy came under the influence of the doctrine of *despotisme éclairé*, which propagated the idea of a new peaceful international order, based on the fraternity of individuals and nations.

These theories of the Physiocrats did not remain completely unopposed, even within their own ranks; their letters often mirror the feeling that it was not exactly easy, in the sixties and seventies of the eighteenth century, to proclaim the advantages of despotism, even though it were enlightened. To counteract this antagonism, the advocates of despotism pointed to Frederick the Great, and even more to Catherine II, who, in the first years of her government, had aroused great hopes when she convened a reform commission and made contacts with some of the leading Physiocrats.

Side by side with this French doctrine, the followers of which were avowed adherents of Enlightened Despotism, the ideas advanced by the eighteenth-century writers on administration in Germany deserve attention in the history of Enlightened Absolutism. Though they were not familiar with the term itself, their principles rested on the same basis. However, their ideas were not so revolutionary as those of the Physiocrats; they had their origin in the writings of the German Cameralists of the sixteenth and seventeenth centuries, from which they gradually developed as the German territorial states took shape, emerging as a distinctive contribution at the time of the eighteenth-century Enlightenment.

Christian Wolff was the first to introduce the ideas of the Enlightenment into German administrative theory, which before his time had been based largely on practical experience and on biblical precepts. His *Vernünftige Gedanken vom gesellschaftlichen Leben der Menschen*, first published in 1721, contains already the principal points of the programme that was to become characteristic of Enlightened Absolutism in Germany. His ideas derive from the Enlightenment in so far as his point of departure is the individual, upon whom he confers specific " rights of man ". The State is a voluntary contract between individuals, and the " furtherance of common welfare and security " is the purpose of the State. At the same time free rein is given to Absolutism, since the individual has no means of forcing the State to observe his rights. On the contrary, because the State has the duty to plan and implement " measures serving to further common welfare and security ", it has the right to insist that its citizens obey its orders. And it is emphasized that they are bound to do willingly whatever the authorities deem to be right. For the practical implementation of these principles Wolff drew up a detailed programme, which Dilthey[9] very appropriately called a manual for the almighty police-state. " It was ", he said, " the greatest intensification and extension of the power of the State since Plato and the first exponents of socialist ideals ", and its basis was the duty of the State to ensure the realization of the common good.

These ideas were expounded and elaborated, without adding anything new, by the German political theorists of the eighteenth century, and particularly by the followers of Wolff, who concentrated on the police duties of the State and liberated administrative doctrine from the narrow concentration on the financial interests of the princes, which the Cameralists had emphasized. The leading representatives of this doctrine— i.e. men like Justi, Sonnenfels and Martini—showed an increasing tendency towards reform, as the influence of the Enlightenment grew; but they still retained the conviction that man had not yet come of age and should therefore be forced to accept and do what was good for him. This tendency reached its climax towards the end of the century, by which time its aim was to hold the citizen in tutelage from the cradle to the grave, and even there to pursue him with princely orders and regulations. The Halle professor G. F. Lamprecht, in his *Versuch eines vollständigen Systems der Staatslehre* (Berlin, 1784), which he prefaced with the quotation from Cicero: " Commodum et felicitas populi prima omnium legum ", set the State the task of making " the citizens in every regard more well behaved, healthier, wiser, wealthier and more secure ", and of procuring them " the comforts and amenities of life ". How far this humane programme led him in the regimentation of life, may be illustrated by a few of his suggestions: all towns, so far as possible, are to be of the same size; roads and streets are to meet at right angles; colouring of Easter eggs is to be prohibited; and mothers are to be compelled to suckle their children. Nevertheless, the ultimate goal for Lamprecht is still the welfare of the citizen and the " furtherance of his bliss ". Th. Kretschmann, on the other hand, definitely puts absolutism first: speaking of his own age, when " reason does not yet commonly govern human actions " and when the " individual refuses to sacrifice himself for the good of the species ", he pictures the State as a kind of " reformatory ", the task of which it is " to lead man through the sacrifice of all his individuality to a higher level of development ".[10]

In practice Enlightened Absolutism was certainly not so radical. The Physiocrats never got beyond the initial stages in the implementation of their doctrines. Although one of their representatives, Turgot, attained the position of Comptroller-General of Finances, thus becoming the director of France's economic policy, he was unable to ensure that any specific elements of the reform programme were carried into effect against the opposition of the privileged classes, which included in this instance the wealthy upper ranks of the bourgeoisie; and, to his own misfortune and that of his country, the king, Louis XVI, was anything but an Enlightened Despot. Among the other monarchs of the period Margrave Charles Frederick of Baden was in correspondence with leading Physiocrats and set about putting their theories into practice. A permanent result of this was the abolition of serfdom in Baden, but his attempt to make land-tax into the only tax—in accordance with the theory of the " impôt unique "—was doomed to failure. In any case, in view of the smallness of his State, his experiment was without general significance.

The contacts which Catherine II of Russia made with the French adherents of Enlightenment—including advocates of the doctrine of *Despotisme éclairé*—might have been more important; but they had almost no practical effect on her government. In certain details, e.g. the foundation of an economic society in 1765, the influence of the Physiocrats can be traced; but the well-known instruction for the Zemstvo or Meeting of Deputies in 1767, the outlines of which were drawn up by Catherine herself, in no way bears the hall-mark of *Despotisme éclairé*, but is based mainly on Montesquieu, although, in view of Russian conditions, it rejects his ideal of a limited monarchy, and pronounces itself in favour of absolutism; its main ideas are those of the Enlightenment, but not those of the Physiocrats. The same may be said of the reforms which the empress introduced in the field of administration.

Thus, the French doctrine of *Despotisme éclairé* remains an interesting trend of thought, but its practical effect was almost nil. I am also inclined to think that it would be a mistake to rate too high the direct influence of the German eighteenth-century administrative theory which has been described above. It is, of course, possible that a certain number of officials in the German bureaucracies were stimulated by lectures they had heard at the University, though no documentary evidence of this can be found in the archives. On the other hand, the possibility cannot be ruled out that many of the demands for reform made in the manuals were the result of practical experience. Therefore, all one can really say about the theoretical basis of Enlightened Absolutism—as it manifested itself in many European states in the second half of the eighteenth century, and particularly in the peaceful years between 1763 and 1792—is that it was founded on the wide propagation of ideas current during the Enlightenment. But that is really all that was needed. Pirenne[11] was right when he pointed out that, after all, Enlightened Absolutism was nothing particularly new, that it was only a new version of the old conception of the prince as the father of his country, with the sole difference that his conduct which had hitherto been influenced by the heart, was now influenced by reason.

On the other hand it would, in my view, be a mistake to

begin the series of monarchs who are regarded as typical representatives of Enlightened Absolutism with Frederick William I of Prussia and still more with Peter the Great of Russia. Of course one should not evaluate Frederick William's relations to learning solely on the basis of the abusive cabinet order in which, on pain of death by hanging, he ordered Christian Wolff to leave Prussia. On the other hand, one should not overrate the intellectual ties connecting Frederick William's work with Wolff and Wolff with Frederick William. How small Frederick William's esteem for scholarship was, is apparent not only in the angry impulse underlying his cabinet order about Wolff; the Prussian Academy of Sciences also experienced it, and it is evident in the pride with which the king, in his instruction to the General-Directory, emphasized that his principles of political economy were derived not from books, but from " experience ".

For these reasons it seems to me that it is still correct to start the series of Enlightened Despots with Frederick the Great. His views of the nature of the State have been discussed so often and so thoroughly that there is little new to be said about them. His idea of the State lacks originality, and simply reflects the theory of the social contract voluntarily entered into between initially free and equal individuals. Even his often quoted description of the prince as " the first servant of the people "[12] can be traced back to antiquity. However, Frederick is the first monarch who not only used these words but put them into practice throughout his reign. Here again, a short survey without details will suffice. In the first place, there is his attitude towards religion, the secularization of the State and the disestablishment of the Church, leaving everybody free to achieve his own salvation in his own way, which did more to enhance his prestige in the eyes of his enlightened contemporaries than his military exploits ever did. His attitude towards law and legal procedure also reflected to the full the principles of the Enlightenment; but in this sphere more than in others he naturally relied on the advice of experts, such as Cocceji or Carmer. Nevertheless, the way he expounded these questions in his political testaments proves that he had given them much thought, and that he recognized the right of his subjects to rapid decisions and impartial jurisdiction. In his financial administration too the influence of enlightened thought is manifest; not only in details—e.g. when, in contrast with his father's practice, he subordinates the interests of the royal budget to the common interest of the country—but also in his acknowledgment of the principle that the king was not the owner, but only the administrator of the wealth of the country, and had no right, therefore, to dispose of it arbitrarily. How far these ideas conflicted with those of his father is apparent from a comparison of the edict concerning the royal domains, which Frederick William had issued in 1713, with the paragraphs on the same subject contained in the Common Law of the Land (*Allgemeines Landrecht*) which, although promulgated by Frederick William II in 1794, had been prepared and publicly debated in the closing years of Frederick the Great's reign. Frederick William I thought of the royal domains as merely a part of the heirloom of the house of Hohenzollern,[13] whereas the *Allgemeines Landrecht* described them as the " property of the State ", from which the monarch is entitled solely to draw " certain revenues and services ". Here the State, as the permanent organization, is deliberately set above the mortal person of the monarch.

There is, however, nothing essentially new in this. The current opinion that the modern State, as a creation of the ruler, was regarded first and foremost as his private affair, that —ever since Machiavelli—" stato " had meant solely the prince and his immediate following, and that only at the time of the Enlightenment was the State regarded as a community which fused the monarch and his people into one unity, is too much of a generalization. In the petty territorial states of Germany a conception of the State as a political entity could not develop—they were too insignificant—and the same was still true in Prussia in the time of the Great Elector and of Frederick William I.[14] But already in sixteenth-century France a clear dividing line was drawn between the *ordonnances des rois* and the *ordonnances du royaume*, and in the critical situation of 1589 Bodin made a point of calling himself " le procureur du publicq et de l'estat royal et non du roi ". In seventeenth-century France this conception of the State was occasionally obscured by the theory of divine right, but it was never entirely discarded. Even Louis XIV, although the opposition unjustly complained that the State counted for nothing and the king for everything in his policy, not only never pronounced the famous words " L'Etat c'est moi ", but on the contrary, he specifically acknowledged the principle of the sovereignty of the State in an utterance made on his deathbed, which has only recently become known: " Je m'en vais, mais l'Etat demeurera toujours ".[15]

Nevertheless, it will always remain Frederick the Great's merit that he made this conception of the State his own, and that, in doing so, he gave to Prussia's higher bureaucracy an immutable standard for their work which enabled them to continue to govern on absolutist principles until 1848, although the leadership of the monarchy failed after Frederick's death.

The subordination of the ruler to the State did not, however, imply a diminution of the absolute power of the Crown. Even in the Prussian *Landrecht* all rights and obligations of the State were vested in the monarch, whose powers of legislation and taxation were unrestricted by parliamentary institutions; and the monarch used his rights in the spirit of tutelage, characteristic of the police state, which reserves itself the right to regulate all external activities of the citizen according to the needs of the State. But although " the natural freedom and the rights of the citizen were not to be restricted more than was necessary for the common purpose ", we reach, at this point, the limits which even Frederick's Enlightened Absolutism dared not transgress. It was not simply that the principle of authoritative leadership was maintained; for most of the theoretical writers admitted that this would have to continue at least until such times as the immature citizen had reached political maturity. The decisive point was that this leadership did not dare—either in the Prussian *Landrecht* or in administrative practice—to attack the existing division of society into Estates or classes determined by birth. In the *Landrecht* it was recognized that this division had become obsolete in view of the development of the modern State; it was expressly stated that the law was binding " for all members of the State, without regard to status, rank or sex ", and that every inhabitant was entitled to claim the protection of the State for his person and his property. On the other hand, it was not thought incongruous to grant the aristocracy prerogatives denied to the other classes; to include all laws dealing with trade, exchange, shipping and insurance, in the section devoted to " The

Bourgeoisie "; and, finally, to maintain to the full the aristocracy's proprietary rights over the person and possessions of the
peasant.

In Frederick's time this discrepancy between enlightened
theory and obsolete practices was certainly caused—for the
most part at least—by the requirements of power politics.
Prussia being one of the youngest and weakest of the Great
European Powers, its position was too insecure for the king to be
able to expose the State to the upheavals which would surely
have resulted from a radical break with the traditional agrarian
system based on hereditary serfdom; not only the finances of
the State, but also the army were closely linked with it, and
would have been affected.

However, side by side with this " imperative of political
necessity ", as Meinecke called it, Frederick's own personal
character influenced him in stopping short of the logical
consequences of the enlightened principles he professed. This
is evident in spheres where reason of state had little importance,
e.g. in educational policy. Dilthey once warmly praised
Frederick's educational policy. " It is a wonderful prospect ",
he said, " without parallel in history, to see how in this Prussian
State all enthusiastically co-operated, how the king, his officials,
preachers, teachers and writers all worked together for one
common goal—the education of the people by their enlightenment."[16] Nevertheless, it cannot be denied that even after
1763 Frederick was personally little interested in the furtherance
of public instruction in Prussia. The reason for this was not
lack of time, but because he cared little for the instruction of
the broader masses, although there are some passages in his
writings, where, in principle, he declared himself in favour of
the diffusion of enlightenment, or where he at least rejected
the view that it was easier to rule over an ignorant people. But
at the bottom of his heart he did not share the optimism felt by
most of the upholders of the Enlightenment, who hoped that
the spread of knowledge and the elimination of prejudice would
bring about the moral progress of mankind; on the contrary,
he became ever more convinced of the incorrigible baseness of
the " maudite race " of men. Therefore his own contribution
to the upsurge of intellectual life which took place in Prussia
during the second half of his reign, lay not so much in active
furtherance as in the general impetus which resulted from his

renown, and in the fact that he did nothing to prevent or restrict it, so that for a time Berlin became the centre of the Enlightenment in Germany.[17]

On the other hand, Frederick's personal attitude had a definitely restrictive influence in the sphere of political economy. He was not without ideas on this subject and his views on progressive income-tax, outlined in the political testament of 1768, are positively modern. However, it is unlikely that he ever systematically studied the various aspects of economics, or that he ever took notice of the newer views of the Physiocrats, since he was very conservative in what he read and was little interested in new publications.[18] In practice, in any case, he never departed from the tradition of mercantilism handed down to him by his father; his handling of it was somewhat more supple, perhaps, but on the whole essentially the same. That meant that he continued to employ the system of prohibitions and tariffs since, in his opinion, the only means of compelling his subjects to produce goods at home was to prevent them from obtaining them from abroad. It seems as if the idea that different times might call for different measures, had scarcely occurred to him, in spite of the fact that the strict enforcement of mercantilist principles gradually made trade so difficult that all parties suffered thereby. When his Ministers cautiously raised the question he was quite capable of snubbing them brusquely and offensively, without even deigning to consider their arguments.

Particularly noteworthy is Frederick's attitude towards the peasantry. He was well aware of the contradiction between his theory of the natural equality of men and the actual situation of the peasants; but he did nothing to change it, or even to alleviate it to any noticeable degree. Even on the royal domains his reforms—apart from a more effective supervision of the tenants—remained limited to one major change: in 1777 the precarious tenure of the serfs was made hereditary, i.e. at the death of a peasant his holding no longer reverted to the crown, but remained the inheritance of his kin. But for the peasants who lived on the lands of the Junkers nothing at all was done: the cabinet order of 1763 which had decreed the abolition of serfdom in Pomerania was never put into effect, in spite of the strong language in which it was drafted (it was to be implemented "implicitly and without argument"). The protection afforded to the peasantry by the crown was effective only in so far as it forbade the manorial lords to annex peasant land, thus protecting—in the interests of the army for which recruits were needed—the peasant class as a whole, but not the individual peasant.

It seems to me that this reserve where the welfare of the peasantry was concerned is another instance of the importance of Frederick's own personal attitude, which always carried great weight in determining his policy. It expresses his marked preference for the aristocracy, which was matched in his character by an equally marked contempt for the broad masses of the people. In this respect he swung Prussian absolutism away from the line it had followed since its beginnings under the Great Elector; it no longer sought to restrict the pretensions of the nobility. It is true that the struggle with the nobility—a struggle which Frederick William I had fought with all his energy—had become unnecessary once they had submitted to royal absolutism and had accepted the duty of service as officers in the army. Nevertheless the preference for the aristocracy which, from Frederick the Great's time onwards, was the policy of almost every Prussian king, was in the long run disastrous for the State.

Thus, in spite of his enlightened ideas, Frederick was not a pioneer who might have led his State into a brighter future, but rather was the last in the line of absolute monarchs. This does not mean that I wish to disparage the positive results of his reign. I shall not speak in this connexion of his foreign policy, since this would lead us too far from our present theme, particularly as the many questions posed by the catastrophes of 1918 and 1945 cannot be dealt with in a few words. If, in my examination of Frederick's internal policy, I have drawn attention above all to the limitations of his political practice, I would still acknowledge its lasting achievements. The mercantilist orientation of his economic policy constituted, in the course of time, an ever growing hindrance, which was widely felt and criticized. But the very existence of this criticism is a sign that his policy had the effect of arousing new forces and educating them. If Frederick did not realize this, and did not perceive that the question was now how best to give these new forces room in which to become active, this failure can be explained and excused by his age, which prevented him from noticing the new trends. It should also be said that the much vilified bureaucracy was not—as is sometimes alleged—fossilized in all its branches, but, so long as the old king reigned, it had no chance to make its voice heard. A new era had arisen, an era which rejected not only arbitrary absolutism, but also (and specifically) the enlightened, benevolent, tutelary form of absolutism. The names of Kant and Humboldt are sufficient evidence of this. Frederick's achievements are undeniable—just as undeniable as the fact that with these achievements absolutism had completed its task.

We shall reach a similar conclusion if we investigate the impact of Enlightened Absolutism on the smaller German principalities. For many years there has been a tendency to exaggerate Frederick's influence over his princely contemporaries, and the effects it had on their methods of government. There is certainly a marked difference between the type of German prince prevalent in the first half of the eighteenth century—the princes whom Frederick in his youth had castigated in his *Anti-Macchiavelli*, rulers who were only anxious to emulate Louis XIV, to build their Versailles, kiss their Maintenon, and parade an army—and the serious-minded princes, both secular and ecclesiastical, caring for the welfare of their subjects, who were numerous from 1763 to the outbreak of the revolutionary wars, or even until the downfall of the Holy Roman Empire in 1806. But precisely where sources still exist to prove Frederick's direct influence, as in the *Fürstenspiegel* which he wrote for Charles Eugene of Württemberg, we find that it failed to produce the anticipated effect. Furthermore, the tasks of the other German princes of that period were entirely different from those that fell to the ruler of the Prussian State, so that Frederick's example can hardly have provided more than a general impulse—an admonition to place themselves at the service of the State. The decisive momentum, however, was provided not by Frederick's influence but by the whole movement of thought and spirit which infused Germany in the course of the Enlightenment. To make use of this movement in order to raise the mental and moral level of their peoples, was a task sufficient to enlist the interests and energies of the more able of the princes, and to re-arouse their feeling of duty—a feeling which sprang from religious roots and had been characteristic of the German princes of the sixteenth century. But apart from the case of Margrave Charles Frederick of Baden, whose connexions with the Physiocrats have already been mentioned, there is little to show that any of them had been influenced by the particular doctrines of Enlightened Absolutism.

Absolutism remained the form of government—absolutism as it had developed after 1648, often in a moderated form and sometimes even without the abolition of the existing Estates and the institutions springing from them. What was new was the spirit that animated it; W. H. Bruford has very aptly called it "benevolent despotism".[19] The starting point of this benevolent absolutism was the conviction that the State had the right, and even the duty, to compel its immature subjects by a profusion of regulations to lead a life governed by reason, for their own and the common good. It discouraged people from entering professions that were saturated and strove to prevent unnecessary display, e.g. by fixing the amount that might be spent on mourning and on wreaths. The very smallness of their territories made it difficult for the enlightened princes to take steps to improve the economic condition of their lands. It was, unfortunately, very true, when J. Möser wrote that the smaller states consisted only of frontiers. There was thus no basis for the intensive promotion of trade and industry in the spirit of mercantilism. Even the extension of the road-system was severely hampered by the narrowness of the frontiers, since frequently enough the neighbouring country was not only unwilling to continue the road through its own territory, but deliberately obstructed commercial intercourse. Economic reforms therefore concentrated mainly on improving agrarian conditions, and many practical results were achieved, e.g. the change from the traditional three-field rotation to new agricultural methods, by which land instead of lying fallow was used for growing fodder, thus improving the conditions for raising cattle. But hardly anything was done to modernize the social order in the countryside; the abolition of serfdom in Baden remained an isolated case, and the commutation of predial services was limited to a few isolated instances.

In spheres where the ruler of even a small principality was his own master, reforms were more extensive. In particular, the educational systems thrived under the care of benevolent governments, even though the finances were usually insufficient for putting all the fine plans for reform into effect, e.g. raising the emoluments of teachers and also their intellectual level by the foundation of training colleges. Religious tolerance, engendered by the spirit of the Enlightenment, often encountered strong opposition from the population itself—for instance, in the case of employment of Catholic officials in Protestant countries, and vice versa—but it was usually possible to carry it through by promising that a particular incident should not form a precedent. Much attention was given also to the improvement of legal procedure. A codification of the existing law, such as occurred in Prussia, and somewhat later in Austria, was beyond the capabilities of the smaller states; but many defects in the penal system were remedied, and closer supervision of the law-courts resulted in better legal protection for the subjects.

To ensure the well-being of the latter was the principal aim of the reforms in the smaller German principalities in the era of the Enlightenment, and in accordance with this aim public welfare was universally accorded a high place in administration. The object was to make the subject " free, wealthy and well behaved ", but now this was to be achieved by positive measures, and not by restrictions and prohibitions, such as are found in the old *Landesordnungen*, i.e. the enactments issued in the sixteenth century by various princes to keep their subjects from harm and prevent them wasting money. One of these new and positive measures was the introduction of insurance against all the common misfortunes of every-day life. In fact the only form of insurance that proved durable was the insurance of buildings against fire, since the State, by compelling all house-owners to join, created a sufficiently broad basis to guarantee the payment of indemnification, which sometimes was passed on to the policy-holders. But experience was not yet sufficient to make possible the creation of a solid basis for establishing accident insurance and pensions for widows and orphans. Existing schemes of this kind were based on voluntary membership, and usually soon ended in failure. It was contrary to the spirit of Enlightened Absolutism to make membership compulsory. A kind of rudimentary National Health Service was also very much hampered by this reluctance to interfere with the private life of the individual. It is characteristic, for example, that the Faculty of Medicine in Jena rejected compulsory vaccination in 1801, on the grounds that it was " irreconcilable with the unassailable liberty which is the right of every father ", and that its view was approved by the Weimar Government.[20]

This discrepancy between the unwillingness of the State to intervene in practice and its theoretical claim to exercise tutelage over its subjects was one of the main reasons why the reforms never became really effective. None of the enlightened " Despots " ever made a serious attempt to draw the consequences from his enlightened principles and to break through, or at least to sweep aside, the barriers of the existing social order. Even when they had decided upon, and ordered the implementation of a reform, the majority of the princes failed to follow it up with the necessary firmness. The result was that the reforms were often only superficially carried out, since the majority of officials were loath to shoulder the burden of new tasks and to give a lead to the population in putting new measures into effect. When, in the *Briefe über die Verfassung der Markgrafschaft Baden*, published in 1786, the anonymous author, an official in the Baden administration, asked: " What is the use of the most excellent decrees, if nobody obeys them? ", his question was amply justified.

This flagging of energy and relaxation of authority was not peculiar to the petty German territorial states only; it was a sign of the times. In Prussia it is very noticeable between 1786 and 1806, and especially after the accession to the throne of the benevolent and enlightened Frederick William III. It looks as if the sincere desire to make the people happy had crippled the energies necessary for powerful action—as if the creative forces of absolutism had become exhausted.

Nevertheless the era of Enlightened Absolutism had important results in German history. The mere fact that many of the German princes—instead of indulging in a misconceived imitation of Louis XIV, living entirely for their own pleasure and squandering the wealth of the country—were, on the contrary, seriously bent on promoting the happiness and alleviating the misfortunes of their subjects, did much to consolidate the position of the monarchy in Germany. The cry of " Liberty and Equality " and the slogans of the French Revolution found an echo only in the minds and hearts of the intellectual classes, but the broad mass of the people remained untouched by them.

As J. Droz recently put it,[21] " they entirely lacked the ambition to emulate the French Third Estate and to become *un tout* ".

There was only one German monarch whose energy was not crippled by benevolence: Joseph II. For this reason his government deserves special mention, quite apart from the size and importance of the territory over which he ruled. He was imbued with the ideas of the Enlightenment and carried them to such extremes that, as Valsecchi has observed,[22] they became revolutionary. He was not content with developing his ideas on paper; he thought it his duty as sovereign to put them into effect in all the lands under his rule, in order to render his people happy. For a long period—which he bore with impatience—he was co-regent with Maria Theresa; and after her death he had only a short decade at his disposal, in which to realize his programme.

His procedure was entirely that of an absolute monarch. Sovereignty, to him, meant unrestricted power, which he had the right to use arbitrarily according to the dictates of " le bon sens et la réflexion ". Traditional fetters, " les thèses tirées du siècle passé et d'un usage de cent années ", held no validity for him. He refused to acknowledge the separate constitutions of the various countries that constituted his heirloom, and for this reason he refrained from being crowned as king of Hungary. It is true that he laid great emphasis on the subordination of the monarch to the State, and stressed the ruler's obligation to administer properly the country's wealth as the property of the State and not his own. But only to God was he prepared to render account; interference by the Estates he would not tolerate. Both his political principles and his personal character led him to concentrate the ruling power in his own person, and to organize the administration of his lands on as uniform a pattern as possible, without consideration for the old frontiers and for variations in the character and constitution of the different provinces and countries. At the same time the traditional local self-government of districts and towns was abolished.

It is unnecessary to follow Joseph's rule in all its ramifications. Only the main spheres require mention, in the first place his Church policy. It has recently been pointed out that this policy was not initiated by Joseph himself, but had already been introduced in Maria Theresa's reign, principally by Kaunitz;[23] but Joseph went much further than his predecessor when, true to the spirit of the Enlightenment, he granted tolerance to the Protestants, and, opposing the Catholic church, insisted on the absolute supremacy of the State over the Church. This attitude was reflected not only in the rearrangement of the administrative organization of the church to bring it into conformity with the frontiers of the different countries, but also in the incisive measures he took with regard to ecclesiastical institutions, in particular the monasteries. This so-called Josephinism has had a far-reaching significance in Austria's history.

The abolition of serfdom was another of Joseph's permanent achievements, although it did away only with personal bondage, leaving in existence the services due to the lord, although they were regulated and could be commuted for rent in kind or money.

Yet even these moderate reforms met with opposition, which grew when he attempted to reorganize the constitution and administration of the State; and Joseph was unable to impose his will and make permanent headway against this opposition. The reason for this lay partly in his own character. Anxious to keep all the threads in his own hand, he was overburdened with details; he did not understand how to make his officials work for him to good purpose and constantly upset the normal channelling of work by issuing special orders and instructions. Patience was not his strongest feature; he would begin many matters simultaneously, and was incapable of waiting quietly for the slow maturing of success. He was never willing to consider criticism, and clung to the decisions he had taken with an unyielding stubbornness which was already compared by contemporaries to the policy of the Stuarts.

The decisive fact, however, was that Joseph's Enlightened Absolutism overshot the objects and overstrained the possibilities of State interference. Not only was it contrary to all tradition when Joseph wished to make of his states " une province égale dans toutes les dispositions et charges "; it was also irreconcilable with the inner structure of the Habsburg monarchy. Hence opposition was not confined to those classes which feared for their prerogatives, but also secured the backing of the broad mass of the people. This opposition was not purely reactionary in character; on the contrary, it marked the first awakening of national feeling when Hungary rebelled against the imposition of German as the official language, and prepared to fight for its ancient constitution.

Joseph was incapable of recognizing the element of justification behind this resistance. To him it seemed proof of the foolishness of the people when the Estates of Brabant rebelled against him, because he wanted to grant them exactly what, at the very same time, the French people were tumultuously claiming as their rights.[24] But it was precisely the fact that Enlightened Absolutism in its ultimate phase swept aside all barriers of tradition, and threatened to lead to revolutionary changes in the life and organization of the State, that gave force to the resistance against Joseph II's rule. The time had passed when subjects meekly complied with all orders given by authority. Confronted by the ceaseless activity of their emperor—who, in the decade when he was sole ruler, overwhelmed them with more than 6,000 orders and decrees, in the attempt to realize an abstract utilitarian ideal—they took refuge in their time-honoured and well beloved customs and usages; they defended their ancient rights all the more sturdily since they believed these rights to be an indispensable protection against the absolute power of government, and since they were afraid that Enlightened Absolutism—though at that particular time it reflected the policy of a benevolent monarch—might easily lead one day to absolute tyranny.

Under the pressure of unrest in the Netherlands and in Hungary, and of the unfortunate Turkish war, into which his restless ambition had led him, Joseph was forced—a short time before his death—to revoke the majority of his reforms. His life-work was wrecked and was never resumed by his successors. Nevertheless, it seems to me an exaggeration to call him the " enfant terrible " or a caricature of Enlightened Absolutism,[25] and I would prefer to speak of his tragic fate. Moltke was aware of this when, in 1831, he said: " This Austrian emperor, to whom history still owes rehabilitation, attempted to achieve by means of the authority and power vested in him, what the French Revolution only obtained after many years of blood and terror ".[26] The tragedy of his failure —as I see it—lies not only in the fact that he succeeded to the throne in a state that was not yet ready to sustain his reforms, but also in himself and his inability to carry through the task he had set himself.

It is not my intention to discuss in detail the other European countries which experienced the influence of Enlightened Absolutism, since it seems improbable that new features can be detected in any of them. In the most important regions of Italy, in Lombardy and in Tuscany, Enlightened Absolutism shows the same characteristics as in other countries under Habsburg rule; and the result there—at least in the territories under Joseph's direct control—was the same as that produced by Joseph's rule elsewhere; in other words, the tension created by striving to increase the power of the State resulted in an estrangement between the dynasty and its subjects which was to play a significant part in the Risorgimento.[27]   According to Valsecchi, even the rule of Leopold of Tuscany—which was much more circumspect and showed in its constitutional objectives a number of modern features pointing forward to the nineteenth century—was resented by the Italian people as alien and un-Italian, a " cold wind from the North ". Whether Leopold, who was convinced that the Age of Absolutism was past, and that it was a wretched business to be a sovereign, should be classed with the Enlightened Despots at all, is another question.

Enlightened Absolutism was also introduced into the states of the Spanish peninsula during the second half of the eighteenth century. In Portugal, it assumed a special character through Pombal's energetic fight for the supremacy of the State over the Catholic church; but in the economic field it remained without permanent results. A survey of the Scandinavian countries also would not add any essentially new traits to the picture we have gained. Denmark probably was the country that came most directly under the sway of Enlightened Absolutism, in the short time Struensee was minister, as well as under the Bernstorffs.

Against this background an attempt may be made to pass judgement on the achievements and the significance of Enlightened Absolutism. Opinions differ widely, even if we leave aside the views of scholars such as G. Lefèbvre, who refuses to consider it as a separate phase of Absolutism at all.

27

Roscher, who tried to distinguish the different phases of Absolutism and classified them in ascending order, regarded Enlightened Absolutism as the highest form, since the " first servant of the State " could dispose far more freely of the wealth and lives of his people than an absolute monarch of the earlier periods would ever have dared to do. This view of Enlightened Absolutism has also been accepted by a number of modern scholars; Valsecchi, for example, recently called it " the topmost point of a parabola ".[28] Koser, on the other hand, believed that the second stage of absolutism was its peak, and that further advance was impossible. Consequently he regarded Enlightened Absolutism as a " retrogression ", in view of " its renunciation of the strict emphasis on the rights of the sovereign, the preponderance given to duties over rights, and the acknowledgment of natural law as the basic principle of monarchy, instead of the revealed divine right, in which seventeenth-century absolutism had seen its guarantee ". In Koser's opinion, however, this did not imply any weakening of the State's claim to power. On the contrary he specifically emphasizes that " in its jealous and suspicious maintenance of its supreme power against all attempts by the subjects to participate in decisions, the absolutism of Frederick II differs in no way from that of Louis XIV, and Enlightened Despotism is no different from un-enlightened despotism ".

The view Marxist historians take of Enlightened Absolutism, as recently expounded by G. Schilfert and H. Krüger,[29] is entirely different. In their opinion it is only the last stage in the development of the feudal state, " the effort of moribund feudal absolutism to keep alive by exploiting bourgeois doctrines and achievements, and thus to retain the control exerted by the feudal class ".

If only the writings of the pure theoreticians are considered —be it the French representatives of *Despotisme éclairé*, or the later Cameralists in Germany, whom we have discussed above —it is easy to gain the impression that Roscher was right when he said that Enlightened Absolutism was a climax which was bound to lead—with all the logic implicit in the doctrines of the Physiocrats—to revolutionary upheaval. But it is only necessary to examine the theory of an active statesman, such as Frederick the Great, to see that this conclusion is subject to considerable limitations. It is true that he still stood for absolutism without control; but, as F. Schnabel has pointed out,[30] the fact that he rationally deduced this particular kind of absolutism from the *Contrat Social* was not merely a check on the self-glorification of the monarch, but, more important still, it signified the eclipse of the idea of a divinely instituted monarchy. If the State was an institution created by the will of man, every man had the right to have his own opinion of it, and his own ideas about improving it. It was therefore only a logical conclusion, when in 1785 the *Berliner Monatsschrift* put forward the view that a prince who wished to secure for his laws long-lasting, if not permanent, validity, had no alternative save to give his State a constitution, " thus making it impossible for his successors arbitrarily to alter the laws he had introduced. He must ensure that henceforth laws could be given only with the consent of the whole State; in short, he must transform the State into a Republic, of which the head of the reigning family is only president."[31] It was in full accord with these conceptions that, about the same time, the higher ranks of the Prussian bureaucracy put forward the claim that since, in the absolute State, they stood in lieu of a constitution, their position should be protected by legal guarantees against any arbitrary decisions of the monarch.

The deliberately simple way of life adopted by monarchs such as Frederick II and Joseph II further helped to deprive the monarchy of its divine nimbus. Looking back, Goethe pointed out that *Sans-culottisme* had been a consequence of this attitude;[32] and it can scarcely be doubted that the inviolability of the monarchy as a divinely ordained institution suffered as a result.

Precisely at the time when the stability of the absolutist régime was being undermined by the secularizing political doctrines of the Enlightenment, the creative energies of the princes (as we have seen above) were on the wane. It had always been a weakness of the system of absolutism that its achievements were so largely dependent on the personal qualifications of the monarch or his ministers. But the fortuitous deficiencies of individual personages were not the only reason for the decline, which is noticeable everywhere, in the energy with which the princes and their ministers tackled their work, and in the practical results they achieved: all symptoms point rather to a flaw in the system. The fact was that it was impossible to get any further with the current system of an almost fatherly tutelage of the subject-population, since this attitude was inconsistent with the very essence of the Enlightenment, which Kant, in a classical phrase, once described as " the liberation of man from his self-engendered immaturity ". Hence it was increasingly opposed by serious thinkers, but opposition manifested itself rather in a withdrawal from political affairs than in an active struggle for spiritual and political freedom. To end this inconsistency by taking an energetic step forward was by now a task beyond the power of Enlightened Absolutism.

I would therefore regard Enlightened Absolutism not as the climax of absolute monarchy, but rather—with Koser—see in it a waning, a last phase. Nevertheless, it is indisputable that it was of great significance, particularly for Germany. But unfortunately " the earnest confidence in German common sense, in ever-progressive true Enlightenment ", on which A. L. Schlözer[33]—who was certainly no uncritical admirer of the princes of his day—thought he could rely " to bring everything to pass that, sooner or later, is bound to happen in Germany, by means of gradual reforms and without revolution ", proved to be unjustified. Nor was the bold assertion made by the Prussian, Struensee, in 1799 that the salutary revolution, which in France had started from the people and surged upwards, would in Prussia start from the top and gradually work downwards, destined to be fulfilled. It is sometimes said to have been a merit of Enlightened Absolutism that it safeguarded Germany from revolution; but this is only superficially true. Though in Germany the revolution did not come from below, it came nevertheless from outside its borders; and, under the pressure of Napoleon's power, Prussia and the states of the Rhenish League were forced to introduce reforms, which they had been reluctant to grant of their own initiative.

It would be tempting to interpret Napoleon's Absolutism as the climax of Enlightened Absolutism, the ultimate phase in which it shed all restrictions. Nevertheless it seems to me that it is something entirely different not only from Enlightened Absolutism, but also from the whole period of " classical " absolutism which lasted from the sixteenth to the end of the eighteenth century. Its precondition was the great French Revolution, from which it derived the prodigious energy, enabling it to throw overboard—without a moment's hesitation —whatever remained of historical ballast. Lack of this energy —it has repeatedly been stated—was the weak point of the enlightened despots. But though it was the driving force which gave impetus to Napoleon's absolutism, at the same time it deprived him of legitimacy, of the self-evident rights of hereditary monarchy, which enabled the older dynasties to weather the severest of storms without being threatened by revolution. For this reason the empire of the Bonapartes— for this applies to Napoleon III as well as to Napoleon I— lacked inner security; it had always to be prepared for a renewed upheaval. Both emperors tried to forestall the danger by establishing pseudo-democratic and pseudo-parliamentary institutions, designed to veil the absolutism underlying them; at the same time, their policy as a whole was deliberately planned to serve the consolidation of the monarchy. Napoleon I sought to win the favour of the masses through a successful foreign policy, while Napoleon III, though in no way renouncing this expedient, tried to forestall revolution by social measures. Thus, although Napoleonic Absolutism took over a number of the characteristics of the absolute monarchies of old, and in some of its features strongly resembled Enlightened Absolutism, it is, nevertheless, something new—namely a manifestation of the era of bourgeois democracy that followed in the wake of the French Revolution. For this reason, therefore, there is in my view every justification for distinguishing between this new type of " Caesarism " and the old system of absolute monarchy in general, and in particular between the Napoleonic régime and Enlightened Absolutism.

NOTES AND REFERENCES

[1] Cf. M. Lhéritier, " Le rôle historique du despotisme éclairé, particulièrement au 18e siècle," in *Bulletin of the International Committee of Historical Sciences*, vol. I (1928), pp. 601–12.

[2] Cf. *Bulletin*, vol. 2, p. 536.

[3] *Ibid.*, vol. 9 (1937), pp. 181–225.

[4] Since Lhéritier's survey little has been published on the general problem of Enlightened Absolutism. Worth mention are: G. Lefèbvre, " Le despotisme éclairé," in *Annales hist. de la Révolution française*, no. 114 (1949), pp. 97–115, and Ch. Morazé, " Finance et despotisme, essai sur les despotes éclairés," in *Annales. Economies-Sociétés-Civilisations*, vol. 3 (1948), pp. 279–96. Every general history of the eighteenth century deals, of course, with Enlightened Absolutism, e.g. C. Hinrichs' section in Rassow's collective work, *Deutsche Geschichte im Überblick* (1953), and L. Just in the *Handbuch der Deutschen Geschichte*, vol. II, section 4. Just there defines Enlightened Absolutism as " a transitional system falling between the era of unrestricted sovereignty—as personified by Philip II and Louis XIV—and the

rise of the national states ". I do not share his opinion, because this definition provides no adequate criteria for classification. R. Mousnier and E. Labrousse also deal with Enlightened Absolutism in their volume *Le XVIIIe siècle* (*Histoire générale des civilisations*, vol. 5, 1953).

[5] This view is shared by R. Mousnier in his report on Absolute Monarchy, prepared for the International Historical Congress held in Rome in 1955 (*Relazioni*, vol. 4, p. 4).

[6] Cf. W. A. Liebeskind, " La Suisse et le despotisme éclairé," in *Bulletin*, vol. 9 (1937), pp. 116–21.

[7] Cf. R. Wittram, " Formen und Wandlungen des europäischen Absolutismus," in *Glaube und Geschichte, Festschrift für Fr. Gogarten* (1948), pp. 278–99.

[8] Cf. G. Lefèbvre, " Le despotisme éclairé," in *Annales hist. de la Révolution française*, no. 114 (1949), pp. 97–115.

[9] Cf. W. Dilthey, *Gesammelte Schriften*, vol. 12 (1936), pp. 183, 195.

[10] Cf. *Hof und Staat*, a periodical edited and almost entirely compiled by Kretschmann (3 vols., 1808–10).

[11] Cf. *Bulletin*, vol. 2, p. 545.

[12] Occasionally, e.g. in his *Anti-Macchiavelli*, Frederick used the expression " premier domestique du peuple ", and the national-socialists, who objected to Frederick's abstract and rationally conceived theory of the State, strove repeatedly to show on the basis of this phrase that Frederick's political thought was developing in a direction which placed greater emphasis on the " folk ". This view was justifiably attacked by E. Schmidt in his book, *Staat und Recht in Theorie und Praxis Friedrichs d. Gr.* (1936).

[13] Cf. O. Hintze in *Forschungen zur brandenburg. u. preuss. Geschichte*, vol. 18 (1905), p. 298, and *Histor. Zeitschr.* vol. 122 (1920), p. 517.

[14] I pointed this out in 1913 in an article on the Political Testaments of the Hohenzollern, printed in *Forschungen zur brandenburg. u. preuss. Geschichte*, vol. 25, and what I said there seems to me still to hold true.

[15] My attention was drawn to it by R. Mousnier's report for the Rome congress (p. 9). F. Olivier-Martin mentions it, without giving his source, in his *Histoire du droit français* (1948), p. 314.

[16] Cf. Dilthey, *Ges. Schriften*, vol. 3 (1927), p. 135.

[17] Cf. H. Brunschwig, *La crise de l'Etat prussien à la fin du XVIIIe siècle* (1947).

[18] This was demonstrated in detail by A. Philippson in an unprinted Berlin dissertation of 1945.

[19] Cf. W. H. Bruford, *Germany in the Eighteenth Century* (1935), p. 11 sq.; but he includes Frederick William I under this heading, since his work was not aimed at his own personal advantage or profit for his following at court.

[20] Cf. F. Hartung, *Das Grossherzogtum Sachsen unter der Regierung Carl Augusts* (1923), p. 101.

[21] J. Droz, *L'Allemagne et la Revolution* (1949).

[22] Cf. F. Valsecchi, *L'assolutismo illuminato in Austria e in Lombardia* (vol. I and vol. 2, part 1, 1931–34); apparently nothing further has been published.

[23] Cf. F. Maass, *Der Josephinismus, Quellen zu seiner Geschichte in Oesterreich*, 1760–1790, vol. 1 (1951).

[24] Cf. M. Lhéritier, quoting Pirenne, in the *Bulletin*, vol. 1, p. 609.

[25] Valsecchi calls him " enfant terrible", *op. cit.*, vol. I, p. 141; " fast eine Karikatur " is the verdict of F. Wagner, *Europa im Zeitalter des Absolutismus* (1948), p. 321.

[26] Cf. R. Stadelmann, *Moltke und der Staat* (1950), p. 67.

[27] Cf. F. Valsecchi's survey of " despotismo illuminato " in the collective work edited by E. Rota, *Questioni di storia del Risorgimento e dell'unità d'Italia* (1951).

[28] Cf. Valsecchi, *op. cit.*, p. 34.

[29] Cf. G. Schilfert in *Zeitschrift für Geschichtswissenschaft*, vol. 1 (1953), p. 784, and H. Krüger, *ibid.*, vol. 2 (1954), p. 796 sqq.

[30] F. Schnabel, *Deutsche Geschichte im 19. Jahrhundert*, vol. 1, p. 51.

[31] The quotation is taken from P. Schwarz, *Der erste Kulturkampf in Preussen um Kirche und Schule*, 1788–1798 (1925), p. 11.

[32] This statement, made in 1810, only became known in 1908; cf. F. Meinecke, *Die Idee der Staatsräson* (1924), p. 421.

[33] Cf. A. L. Schlözer, *Allgemeines Staatsrecht* (1793), p. 166.